BIBLICAL
Sex Education

What the Bible Says About
Cohabitation and Sex Before Marriage

BIBLICAL Sex Education

What the Bible Says About Cohabitation and Sex Before Marriage

Pastor Samuel K. Dorgbetor

BIBLICAL SEX EDUCATION:
What the Bible Says About Cohabitation and Sex Before Mariage

Pr.samueldorgbetor@gmail.com
0202224173/0240695059

Revised in 2021
ISBN: 978-9988-3-0978-7

Cover design by
Nii Armah Aryee
Tel: +233 249714440

Page Layout Design by
Sam K. Nyarko-Mensah
Tel: +233 (0) 269601954

Printed and bound in Ghana by
Yamens Press Ltd.

CONTENTS

to

the Almighty God,
my lovely wife,
children,
family and friends.

ACKNOWLEDGEMENTS

I am very grateful to the Almighty God for making this book a success. I also express my appreciation to my wife, children, family and friends for their support and prayers throughout the writing of this book.

I owe much gratitude to George Meke Kormisah, an Adjunct Lecturer, Valley View University for his assistance, immense contributions and directions during the compilation of this book.

All I can say is, may the good Lord bless you all.

PREFACE

This book is very important because it may unravel some of the subjects taught in sex education in the Christian perspective and its essence with regard to the impact the subject will make on the lives of young people. It will also respond adequately to the sexual moral crisis in Ghana. This study may significantly add to the academic worth of the subject of sex education. More so, it may help to inform churches and their leaders of the need for the church to be involved in sex education and may propose some important activities that the church can include in their sex education programmes to ensure that the gospel itself is preached and sexual moral crisis and decay in the country is adequately addressed.

Finally, this book will help readers to understand Christian sex education and its need in the church for especially young people as well as adults.

It is the parents' God-given responsibility to teach children God's perspective on every area of life, including sexuality

1

HOW SHOULD CHRISTIANS VIEW SEX EDUCATION?

Children will learn about sexuality from someone. The options are their peers, pornography, school settings, experimentation, or their parents. The best place for sex education is in the home, as a natural part of training children "in the way they should go" (Proverbs 22:6). It is the parents' God-given responsibility to teach children God's perspective on every area of life, including sexuality (Ephesians 6:1-4).

Due to the intrinsic complexities of human sexuality, the physical aspects of biological reproduction cannot be separated from moral responsibility. Regardless of whether children receive sex education in schools or even at church, it remains the parents' responsibility to ensure their children are properly educated about both the biological and moral aspects of sexuality. Leaving values-training to others is dangerous, particularly regarding matters of sexuality in many cultures today.

First, what does the Bible say about sex? Sexuality is a gift to us from God and should be viewed as such. God created sex for two purposes: procreation and unity between husband and wife (Genesis 1:28; Matthew 19:6; Mark 10:7-8; 1 Corinthians 7:1-5). Any other use of sex is sin (1 Corinthians 6:9, 18; 1 Thessalonians 4:3). Sadly, many in our world do not believe these truths. As a result, there are many perversions of sexuality and much unnecessary pain caused by them. Parents who properly educate their children about sex can help their children discern truth from error, walk in wisdom, and ultimately have a more wholesome experience of the gift of sexuality.

Most modern sex education instruction presents perversion, fornication, homosexuality, and living together before marriage as "normal" expressions of sexuality. Any teaching of boundaries is limited to the avoidance of negative consequences. All of this is contrary to Scripture (1 Corinthians 6:9; Leviticus 20:15-16; Matthew 5:28). Christian parents should be actively involved in all aspects of their children's education, especially in areas that compromise Scripture. Parents should be aware of what their children are learning and correct any misinformation given to their children. They should also educate their children in such a way as to equip the children to discern biblical truth from cultural error. God holds parents responsible for the upbringing of their children (Ephesians 6:4), not schools, churches, or governments.

Many parents find the topic of sexuality awkward and embarrassing, but it doesn't need to be. Parents should begin when the children are very young, speaking matter-of-factly with pre-schoolers about their bodies and how men and women are made differently. Those conversations transition naturally into more complex areas as the child matures. It is important that a child knows he or she can talk to mum or dad about anything that confuses them.

Sexual information bombards us from every direction, so these parent-child conversations must begin very early. Before parents allow a school system to instruct in sexuality or morality, they must be sure their children have already learned the truth. It is then crucial to stay abreast of what the children are learning and how they are applying their knowledge. Keeping a constant, open dialogue with one's children is a key to staying in charge of what they are learning. When parents are proactive in their children's instruction, those children have a basis upon which to recognise and reject errors that the world promotes as truth.

BIBLICAL APPROACH TO SEX EDUCATION IN CHRISTIANITY

Parents must take the time to talk to their children about sex, or they'll learn about it from the street, so here is a look on sex education from a biblical viewpoint.

SEX EDUCATION

Sex education can be intimidating for parents, yet God created sex as a completely natural aspect of human life. Even so, parents frequently delay talking about sex because they can't seem to find the right time or find the right words, so parents keep putting it off, but this is getting them nowhere. Talking about sex should be completely natural as it lies in the core of human existence. After all, that is how your children were brought into this world, so as soon as they get curious about sex, take the time to talk to them about it.

It should be noted that many teenagers are taught sex education from peers, family, church, etc. casually, therefore it is appropriate the teenagers received formal sex education before they turned 18. Such a high rate suggests that sexuality should be taught correctly, and it should begin early and be within the context of a biblical approach.

SEX AND MARRIAGE

Here are some critical pointers with references to Scripture that talk about sex, marriage, and associated topics to help us better understand the biblical format about the reasons why God created sex.

Marriage and Marital Significance

First Corinthians 7:2 —

> "But because of the temptation to sexual immorality, each man should have his own wife and each woman her own husband."

The Bible promotes being honest with your spouse and having an exclusive relationship. According to the Pew Research Center, cohabitation is on the rise while marriage has significantly declined since the last decade. People with strong religious affiliations now find it acceptable for couples to live together, even if they don't plan on getting married. It should be pointed out that some Christians say it is acceptable to live together without being married.

Ethical and Societal Implications

Leviticus 18:20 –

> "And you shall not lie sexually with your neighbour's wife and so make yourself unclean with her."

Since the Bible promotes exclusivity in relationships, it also discusses the ethical and societal implications of not remaining faithful. It clearly points to having, not only the religious consequences of cheating on your spouse, but moral and ethical dilemmas that would end up having them questioning their own life's choices. It is important to emphasise this: the Bible teaches us to be committed to one partner only, and any sex outside of marriage is sin.

Sexual Immorality

Matthew 15:19 —

> "For out of the heart come evil thoughts, murder, adultery, sexual immorality, theft, false witness, slander."

The Bible highlights the evil and counts sexual immorality amongst those which are major evils or sins. These are among the worst that human beings are capable of committing. It focuses on sexual desire and making people realise that committing sexual immorality of any form may lead them to commit many more atrocities without realising that they have strayed away from the goodness of God, and are now living in disobedience. Sin has a way of deceiving us. What does the Bible say about same sex marriage?

Homosexuality

1 Corinthians 6:9 —

> "Or do you not know that the unrighteous will not inherit the kingdom of God?

> Do not be deceived: neither the sexually immoral, nor idolaters, nor adulterers, nor men who practise homosexuality."

The Bible, no matter how modern it may be perceived, is not in favour of homosexuality. According to statistics published on Statista about homosexuality, one in a hundred women and two in a hundred men identify themselves as homosexual, but many of these people would still mutually identify as religious, perhaps each to his or her own faith, but the Bible is crystal clear on this subject. Even though homosexuality, like all sexual immorality, is an abomination to God, it does not warrant violence on those who practise it. The Bible teaches us to do what is right and not sin, but children should still know that it does exist in the world. Even though most of the world has now generally accepted homosexuality, children still must be taught that it is wrong.

DIVORCE AND ADULTERY

Matthew 5:32 —

> "But I say to you that everyone who divorces his wife, except on the ground of sexual immorality, makes her commit adultery, and whoever marries a divorced woman commits adultery."

According to recent statistics, divorce is on the rise these days. Many women especially are suffering from the problem of effective and proper care for their children because of divorce. Single parenthood is very common as a result of divorce and separation. Therefore, among cultures that practise the material system of inheritance the burden of the child care rest on the mother.

ADMONITION

James 4:17 —

> "So whoever knows the right thing to do and fails to do it, for him, it is sin."

The Bible is a guide given to us by God and is intended to show us how to live a fulfilled, wholesome life more than anything. Hence it is critical for parents to teach their children about sex and about the importance of doing the right thing according to the Bible. Instruct your children about the right to their own body as opposed to the right anyone else should have over their body, be that a stranger, family, or friend, and they can always come to you (the parent) about anything at all, especially when it comes to the question of sex.

The idea about sex should not be treated as if it is a taboo to let children hear of it. Remember in your absence (parents), they will hear and see what you are hiding from them, especially in this computer age.

"Sexuality is not initially a matter of psychology; it is a matter of the nature of humanity itself as created by God, so it is a matter of theology."

2

THE ISSUE OF SEX AND SEXUALITY

The topic of sex and sexuality is of urgent interest to young people in the world since the late 20th century. It is a force which tends to dominate the media yet there seems to be so many diverse descriptions to sex. People have described sexual intercourse as "thrilling, soul-stirring, deeply satisfying, wonderfully comfortable, fascinating, delightful, boring, shocking, and painful, disappointing, disgusting, and so on." According to Lahey (2004), sex could be a transaction without emotional meaning or a loving union, while others state that sex in boy-girl relationship keeps love from growing.

Parker Gagnon (1995) explains sexuality using script theories whereby sexual conduct rests on quite different assumptions about the ways in which specific sexual patterns are acquired and expressed.

First, scriptists assume that patterns of sexual conduct in a culture are locally derived (that is, that what is sexual and what sex means differs in different cultures). Second, they assume that there is no innate sexual instinct or drive and that infants do not possess any information about sex or specific sexual aims when they are born. Infants may vary biologically in activity level and temperament, but there are no direct links between this variation and what they will do sexually as adults. Third, they assume that individuals acquire, through a process of acculturation that lasts from birth to death, patterns of sexual conduct that are appropriate to that culture (including those patterns that are thought to deviate from the norms of the culture). Fourth, they assume that people are not simply mirrors of the sexual scenarios provided by their culture and that as they get older, they make individual adaptations to what is originally provided by the culture. In complex and contradictory cultures, such individual adaptations will be very diverse.

Given these assumptions, people acquire scripts for sexual conduct (who they should have sex with, when they should have sex, where they should have sex with them, what they should do sexually and why they should do sexual things). These scripts embody what the inter-subjective culture treats as sexuality (cultural scenarios) and what the individuals believe to be the domain of sexuality. Individual improvise around the cultural scenarios and in the process of social action create a changed sexual culture for the society. Individual sexual actors as well as those who create representations of sexual life (e.g. the mass media, religious leaders, educators, and researchers) are reproducing and transforming sexual life in a society.

For example, introducing condoms in sexual activity is part of an AIDS education and prevention programme requiring changing scripts for sexual conduct on the part of individuals. If large numbers of individuals use condoms, they will change the health situation around sexuality by reducing AIDS, other sexually transmitted diseases, unwanted pregnancies and abortions. But sex education should be given appropriately, directing the spiritual wellbeing of the youth in the church.

"Sexuality is not initially a matter of psychology; it is a matter of the nature of humanity itself as created by God, so it is a matter of theology." God is spirit, yet he created man with dust and put His spirit in the man (making man similar to God) and from the man's rib created a woman who was similar to man. The mystery of sex is the difference that exist between the similar beings (man and woman) created by God. In the creation dynamics, the woman was taken out of the man but in the sex act the man returns into the woman and they are joined. In this, they are complete in their relationship with the Father, the Son and the Holy Spirit, however this is only when the man and the woman are married.

SEXUALITY AND ADOLESCENCE IN THE EARLY CHURCHES

In the early Christian church, few restrictions were placed on adolescent boys. Kiel (1967) cites a passage from St Augustine's writings that mirror descriptions of adolescent boys today, including mention of sexual curiosity and body changes. It was around sixth century when the church "penitential" were dispersed to govern the sexual conduct of clergy (Gies & Gies 1989). The penitential specified sex only at a certain time of the year and were exclusive to heterosexual marriages. Penalties for other activities, ranging from kissing to oral sex, were severe.

During the middle ages various changes occurred in church and state doctrines governing adolescent sexuality. The church sought great social control over parishioners. This led to restrictive measures governing adolescent sexuality which included bans on premarital sex, homosexuality, masturbation, abortion and contraceptives (Boswell, 1980). There are other evidence to show that the church exerted sexual norms, for example the first systematic persecution of sexual nonconformists and banning of parishioners from direct access to the Bible (Boswell, 1980).

During late 18th century and early 19th century, sexuality study was placed under the direct purview of religion and not science. The Women's Christian Temperance Union (WCTU) of the late 1870s and 1880s attacked all forms of public indecency, including adolescent vices (Kett, 1977). The Young Men Christian Association complemented the WCTU's activities from the 1870s onward and even published scores of pamphlets designed to terrorise adolescents about the evils of sexuality (Kett, 1977). Some religious groups established homes for unwed pregnant adolescents and these girls were kept in groups, homes long after births of their offspring (who were adopted by others) so as to keep them away from additional exposure to worldly vices. In a report by Lancaster (1987) and Starbuck (1899), it was shown that religious leaders and psychologists asserted that the only way to keep adolescents away from sexual activities was religious conversion.

SEXUAL OPENNESS IN THE CHURCH

The contribution of researcher Rijk van Dijk focuses on the Pentecostal movement as a form of Christianity that has become very popular in Africa. In the Seventh-day Adventist Church and in almost all Pentecostal churches, people have strong views about the desired lifestyle of its members, including abstaining from smoking and drinking, and abstinence of sexual relationships outside of marriage. The movement is characterised by an emphasis on charismata; the workings of the Holy Spirit. 'Becoming born again' is essential to the Christian identity. This is expressed in spiritual and social ways by breaking with cultural traditions and ties. The movement is in social-economical terms, a middle-class movement, focused on this-worldly success rather than a good after-life. The movement is matured in the cities of African countries such as Uganda, Zambia, Nigeria and Ghana. The close political ties it has developed are important when trying to understand the social-moral messages of the movement, including its understanding of sexuality.

In almost all churches the nuclear family is actively advocated. The ties with the extended family are diminishing under the influence of this break with the past. This opens up the possibility for religious leaders to exercise moral power over the faithful. Religious leaders are mediators who make sure that social functions, ritual and other obligations are not conflicting with the teachings of the church. Their authority is particularly influential in life events such as birth, marriage and death. The sexual morals that are advocated are strict; sexual relations before marriage are forbidden and young people are expected to follow the practice of abstinence.

Three perspectives on the approaches of sexuality in the Pentecostal movement in Africa Pentecostalism is a movement in the younger generation, in the sense that the authority of elders is not taken for granted. Older generations are often blamed or deemed morally inferior, amongst others because of the critique towards ancestral and traditional spirituality. It is a paradox that the ideology that is conservative in its rules, moral discipline and gender relations, is seen as liberating young people from their ties with older generations. This moral leadership claimed by young people is based on both conservatism and progressivism and therefore is at odds with western presuppositions on conservatism in the Pentecostal movement.

This paradox in the generational perspective is also observed in the gender perspective. Pentecostal churches have a majority of female members, while the leadership is often exclusively male. While the belief is that women can also have charismata and therefore act as spiritual leaders, they are often not able to do so as formal leaders in a church. The paradox in this perspective is that women have excellent opportunities to strive for social and financial success, which influences them to demand higher moral standards of their husbands. In marital counselling sessions, men are prepared to act as responsible husbands, which includes both financial independence as well as emotional involvement in the marriage. Ideas of what it takes to be a good man and husband, change more radically in Pentecostalism than the ideas of a good woman and wife.

The third perspective is the so-called fecundist perspective or the connection between sexuality and reproduction. The strong connection between sexuality and reproduction is characteristic of the Abrahamic religions (Judaism, Christianity and Islam). The Seventh-day Adventist, the orthodox and the Pentecostal churches in particular have strongly advocated faithfulness in marriage and abstinence for youth. This should be seen in the context of the middle-class ideals, and the missionary and Victorian roots of contemporary African views on sexuality. While sexuality has been a taboo subject for a long time, the issue of AIDS has placed sexuality on the agenda of churches. In marriage counselling and in the public space of the church, sexuality is increasingly discussed as positive. Sexuality is openly discussed between people of different age-groups. This reveals another paradox, namely that Pentecostalism that in the AIDS crisis was a conservative power, strongly opposed to liberal sexual morals such as the use of condoms, now are becoming much opened about sexuality than the more traditional Christian churches. This does not mean though, that Pentecostals embrace a more liberal view on sexuality and marital relations. What they do offer is a language and a safe space, to make an open exchange on sexuality between people of different generations and sexes possible.

WHAT CURRENT SEX EDUCATION IS LIKE

Current sex education can often add to the sexualised culture by exposing even children who are protected from inappropriate material by their parents at home to explicit images and discussion topics at school. Even where controversial issues are not raised by the teachers themselves, questions asked by classmates in sex education lessons can expose children to information and discussion beyond what is suitable or age-appropriate.

It is clear from our booklet, Too Much, Too Young, that sex education materials can very easily contribute to, rather than counteract, sexualisation.

SEXUALITY AND SEX EDUCATION

Sexuality is at the core of our human existence. Therefore, we have a responsibility to equip our children with a comprehensive view of sexuality early. As people who believe in God, for sexuality to be taught correctly, it must be taught within the context of a biblically holistic approach and it must take into account the whole person—spirit, mind, and body.

If our children are to have a healthy respect and appreciation for the gift of sexuality, parents must both educate and model the precepts and principles that lead to greater sexual health and integrity.

As for timing and when to get started, there's no time like the present.

PARENTAL RESPONSIBILITY

The special relationship between parents and their children is clearly seen throughout Scripture. The fifth commandment says we are to honour our father and mother (Exodus 20:12; Ephesians 6:2-3). The Bible speaks of children being a gift of God to parents (Psalm 127:3). Parenthood is given by God and parents carry a God-given authority and responsibility for the raising of children (Ephesians 6:4). This God-ordained pattern of parental authority is a general principle applying to all parents and all children.

Christian parents are to teach their children to love God (Deuteronomy 6:4-9), and children are to obey their parents because "this is right" (Ephesians 6:1) and "pleases the Lord" (Colossians 3:20). Children should listen to their father's instruction and not forsake their mother's teaching (Proverbs 1:8).

So, the Bible is clear that parents have the primary responsibility for training their children. Anything that threatens to undermine this is of great concern and must be strongly resisted if Christian parents are to be able to fulfil their God-given responsibilities.

MORAL FRAMEWORK

The Bible provides God-given moral absolutes for personal and social conduct (e.g. Exodus 20:1-17; Mark 12:28-31; 1 Corinthians 6:9-10; Colossians 3:5-9). Christian parents want teaching about sex and relationships to be within that moral framework. All too often, what is taught in schools will be devoid of this. Relationships that are morally wrong, such as same-sex relationships, are put on a par with God-ordained relationships such as traditional marriage.

Christians also believe that living according to biblical standards is good for all people, not just Christians. So Christians are not just concerned about children from Christian homes but about any children in our society being taught about sex and relationships outside the biblical framework.

DUTY TO PROTECT YOUNG PEOPLE

There is a duty to defend the vulnerable and the weak:

> "Speak up for those who cannot speak for themselves, for the rights of all who are destitute. Speak up and judge fairly; defend the rights of the poor and needy" (Proverbs 31:8-9).

Jesus gave a very solemn warning of judgement for those who lead children who believe in him to sin. Jesus said,

> "It would be better for him to be thrown into the sea with a large millstone tied around his neck" (Mark 9:42).

SEX EDUCATION FROM THE BEGINNING

The more I learn of God, the more I appreciate the book of Genesis. Here a solid foundation of God's design for sexuality is presented as our children learn about the Garden of Eden and how God created both male and female and told them to reproduce themselves (Genesis 1:27-28).

As parents, we begin sex education by pointing out how God thought of sex in the first place. He created a man and woman who could participate in his ongoing creation and make babies by loving each other in a special way. God also knew that a man and a woman would grow to desire a special companionship that includes enjoying the differences in each other's bodies. And, although this final point may need to wait until children are able to grasp it, we can teach that God gave the unity found in marital relationship as a sign and symbol of the internal love of the Trinity and His love for us.

So, sexuality provides at least three basic lessons that our children can understand. Sexual union exists:

1. to make babies,
2. to nurture a mummy and daddy's love, and
3. to point us back to the love of the Father, Son, and Holy Spirit.

SEX EDUCATION AS THEY MATURE

This initial lesson can be unpacked further as our children mature. We can teach, for example, that sex is appealing and that it's perfectly normal—especially for teenagers and adults—to want to be sexual with someone of the opposite sex. We should emphasise that God is the One who made us to desire healthy expressions of what it is to be male or female, and that "there is a time for everything" (Ecclesiastes 3:1). This emphasis on timing begins with an affirmation of developmental maturity and sexual desire, and teaches a child that when the time is right, sex will be right.

We'll want to teach a clear message about timing. The right time for sexual behaviours occurs when a man and woman are married. Our younger children only need to hear that God designed sex or sexual intercourse for husbands and wives. As our children mature, they will need to learn that all sexual behaviours are more or less foreplay, leading to the act of intercourse, and that these behaviours are also designed for marriage.

SEX EDUCATION AND CULTURAL MESSAGES

We can also point to various cultural messages about sexuality and develop teachable moments. For example, we can't shelter our children from every lewd poster in the mall or every sensual song played in a restaurant. But we can take these moments to affirm the basic goodness of sexuality because of God's loving design, and then make a comment about what's wrong with how sexuality is misrepresented in the culture. These brief messages will be more impactful when offered in a positive and relational manner. Our messages need to be tied to God's love for us, and how we express our love for Him through obedience.

Children need to learn early that God's plan is healthy and Satan's plan is harmful. In the early years we can talk rather simply of what is good and bad. We want to teach them what to think about sex from the Bible and not just from our personal opinion or experiences. As they mature, we shift our approach and begin to teach them how to think.

SEX EDUCATION: A BIBLICALLY HOLISTIC APPROACH

Much of sex education—even within faith-based communities—misses a foundational point. Sex between a husband and wife symbolises the future marriage between Christ and the Church. And as Christians we are "engaged" to Christ (along with the rest of the Church) when we accept His atonement for our sin. We want our children to understand that the Bible begins in Genesis with the marriage of a man and a woman and ends in Revelation with the marriage of Christ and the Church (Revelation 19:7).

Between Genesis and Revelation, God's Word has numerous lessons about sexuality. For example, we can teach our children the stories of Samson and Delilah (Judges 16:1-21), David and Bathsheba

(2 Samuel 11), the Ten Virgins (Matthew 25:1-13), Rahab the prostitute (one of Jesus' biological relatives through his mother Mary), and the woman caught in the act of adultery (John 8:1-11)—who Jesus loved and redeemed. We can help our children understand the differences between David who looked lustfully at Bathsheba and sinned and Joseph who ran from Potiphar's wife when tempted (Genesis 39).

GOD MADE MALE AND FEMALE

In our teachings we want to be clear that in God's eyes, males and females are equal in worth (Galatians 3:28), and that both have sinned (Romans 3:23). This fact also permits us to share the mercy of God who forgives sin even though painful consequences may remain. For example, David was forgiven and still called "a man after God's own heart" (Acts 13:22), but the baby he and Bathsheba produced in their adultery died (2 Samuel 12:15-17), and one of his sons eventually raped one of his daughters (2 Samuel 13).

We will need to remember that in the early years, our children think in concrete terms rather than abstract terms. These lessons of men and women in the Bible teach cause and effect—sex can produce a child, and one person can tempt or seduce another. What we hope to accomplish is the spiritual formation that includes a healthy view of sexuality and heart-felt respect for males and females. We want our children to connect their sexuality with God's design for life and peace.

SEX EDUCATION: PRECEPTS AND PRINCIPLES

No two children are alike—even in the same family. We will want to be sensitive to how our children are developing physically, mentally, emotionally, and spiritually. We also want sex education to occur in both spontaneous and structured moments.

As our children continue to mature, we'll want to help them understand that God really is for us (Romans 8:31), and that His plans are designed to benefit us (Jeremiah 29:11-13). We'll also want them to understand the difference between a precept (a stated do or don't) and a principle (the general application of a truth that requires reason and discernment).

Sex education precepts

Take, for example, the seventh commandment, “Do not commit adultery” (Exodus 20:14). This command is an example of a precept. It clearly states what not to do. So we will want our children to learn this precept and others, and the right time to learn these important life lessons long before they’re tempted.

Sex education principles

We will also want our children to be able to connect the dots. For example, the Bible doesn’t say, “Thou shalt not view Internet pornography.” But various principles are given to us. We are to avoid lust with our eyes (Matthew 5:27-28 and 1 John 2:15-17), and that principle leads us to conclude that we should avoid Internet pornography or any other form of sexual behaviour based on lust.

Far more important than the behaviours, however, is the physicality of being male and female (Genesis 5:2). By principle, we can teach our sons they are to be a type of Christ to their future wives. His kind of sacrificial love is pure and nurturing, never self-centred, abusive or degrading. Therefore, we need to teach our sons to honour the females in their lives including the girlfriends they relate to prior to marriage.

We can teach our daughters they are to be a type of the Church to their future husbands, preserving their purity and preparing well for the day they and their bridegroom become one. Our daughters need to understand, for example, that dressing provocatively fails to communicate purity and wholesome intentions. By continually teaching the love story that exists between Christ and us, the Church, we can help them to honour and steward sexuality — both theirs and others.

SEXUALITY AND SPIRITUALITY

Teaching sexual health and integrity requires a Christocentric approach. We want our children to learn early that sexuality is a function of our bodies, minds, and spirits. It is so much a part of us that it is impossible to separate sexuality from spirituality. These two facets of our makeup are intricately connected. The Apostle Paul began to speak of marriage between a man and a woman and how these symbolise the marriage between Christ and the Church (1 Corinthians 7:1-16). He also concluded that it was a great mystery (Ephesians 5:31-33).

Our children need to see the mystery of God-ordained sexuality and hold it in awe, just as we do. Our sons as a type of Christ can learn to regard their masculinity and physicality as a sacred trust, and our daughters as a type of the Church can learn to regard their femininity and physicality as an equal and sacred trust. As our children mature, we can teach that sexuality between a husband and wife is a private discipleship where "the two become one flesh" (Genesis 2:24) and are participating in the divine love of God in that moment more than at any other time.

SEX EDUCATION: TIMING

I have to chuckle and think that our concern for timing is more about our comfort than our children's. I mean, let's get real. Look at the world we are living in. Everyone else is talking about sex, so we'd better get started now.

Sexuality is a cradle-to-grave reality, and we have only a few short years to nurture our children's moral development. By learning more about childhood development, we can better time our efforts with God's design. For example, a child's sense of modesty can develop as early as eighteen months. Therefore, this God-given, developmental window is the ideal time to teach and model a balanced, sacred modesty in the home.

SEX EDUCATION: SANCTITY OF SEXUALITY

The first thing about sex education is to get started. Let's teach the sanctity of sexuality. Our children need to learn that God ordained sexuality to be the means in which they—and everyone else—come into existence for all eternity.

We need to understand our children and the difficult culture in which they live. As parents—and hopefully, as older brothers and sisters in Christ—we have the privilege to teach them what we are learning in relationship to God and His plan for the family.

THE BIBLE AND SEX EDUCATION

Untreated cancer almost always means death to the affected individual. There are times when the diagnosis is made too late to institute effective treatment, or it is possible that inadequate measures may spell doom. Fortunately, where an early diagnosis is made and proper procedures are carried out, a high percentage of cures may be expected.

Sex obsession is a moral and spiritual cancer which is designed to destroy us as surely as untreated cancer destroys human life.

The diagnosis is open to all who can see. Our literature, stage, screen, and accepted standards of life literally reek with an obsession about sex that has now reached unbelievable proportions.

Now, there is nothing intrinsically wrong with sex. It is a God-given force in which, within the mutual bonds of wedded love, there is both righteousness and joy.

Our trouble today is that "sex appeal" is in large measure a determining factor in our way of life. It is the promotion of, acquiescence in, and submitting to this godless concept of life that is destroying America.

If this diagnosis be correct—and it is obvious that it is—then our great concern must be the instituting of an effective counterattack.

The basic cure lies in our acceptance of God's standards for sex conduct, and not those of the world.

The Seventh Commandment states categorically: "Thou shalt not commit adultery," and this has never been abrogated.

HOW SHOULD A CHRISTIAN VIEW SEX EDUCATION?

It is critical that we provide our children with Bible-based sex education. Secular culture has perverted God's original design for sex, wreaking havoc on our physical, emotional, and spiritual wellbeing. Children are exposed to sex through media, friends, school-based programmes, and occasionally church-based programmes. While these sources can provide some positive input, more often than not, they base their opinions on what is considered appropriate by culture, not God. Therefore, parents need to take the lead in educating their children so that they are informed and can make choices that will lead to both a healthy and God-honouring future.

Secular sex education comes from schools, media, and friends. School health curriculums teach students about the anatomy and physiology of their reproductive systems and guidelines for having positive romantic relationships. However, the moral perspective can vary greatly from school to school and many places no longer support abstinence, but rather encourage students to explore sexuality in ways that are contrary to the Bible. In addition, public schools cannot teach about sex within the context of God's plan. The media celebrates immoral sexual activity such as sex outside of marriage, transgenderism, and homosexuality. Also, friends provide numerous opinions on sex which can be biased and false.

Church-based sex education can vary as well. Some churches provide positive and biblical insight into sex. Nonetheless, some churches present a negative view of sex focusing on the sinful aspects rather than on how God intended sex to be. In addition, some church programmes use fear and guilt as intimidation tactics to keep children from exploring sex, which can lead to a distorted view of sex in the future.

Ultimately sex education outside the home should be in addition to, not in place of, sex education at home. Although it may be awkward, parents should begin sex education early on, focusing on what is most appropriate at each stage of their child's life. By talking about the realities of the human body, how men and women are made differently, and other matters related to sexuality, parents help their children feel comfortable to come to them with questions and concerns. Their child will be informed of God's true design for sex and be able to discern truth from lies as they encounter sex outside of the home. Parents should also continue to educate themselves as culture evolves and provide children with a positive model of what a healthy relationship looks like.

Not sure where to start? Begin with the Bible. It very clearly outlines God's perspective on sex. God created us man and woman and intended sex to be between a married man and woman (Genesis 2:24; Mark 10:6-9). Sex has three main purposes: procreation, pleasure, and relationship (Genesis 9:7; Song of Solomon; Ephesians 5:31-32). Within the context of marriage, sex establishes a unique human relationship which symbolises our relationship with God.

On the whole, Africans do not regard sex as something evil and hence something to be suppressed, even if it must be kept under control.

3

ATTITUDES OF AFRICANS TOWARDS SEXUALITY

African indigenous culture has no hung-ups about sexuality. It is clear in its affirmation of sexuality, that, it is good, satisfying and blessed. Hence, a mother confirmed this positive attitude towards sexuality when she said, "You sigh with relief when your son experiences his first wet dream or your daughter her first menstruation. For then you confirm that all is normal."

Sexuality in indigenous Africa was looked upon as mysterious and sacred. If misused, evil surely resulted. Sexuality and its powers were understood as permeating every level of human existence. Hence the insistence that, boys behave as male and girls as female. On the whole, Africans do not regard sex as something evil and hence something to be suppressed, even if it must be kept under control.

THE VALUE THAT INDIGENOUS AFRICANS ATTACH TO SEXUALITY

The value that indigenous Africans attach to sexuality can be summarised in the following observation: 'Infidelity and sterility block the channel through which the stream of life flows; they plug the person concerned into misery, sever him/her from personal immortality and threaten the perpetuation of the lineage'. And because the generation of life was a matter of concern to the whole community, there were strong sanctions against people who indulged in sex for selfish reasons.

It follows therefore that in almost all parts and cultures of Africa, all sexual acts that did not fulfil the conditions of marriage and childbearing, were condemned as deviant and severely punished. These are mono-sexual acts such as masturbation, homosexuality, rape and incest. In Iteso culture (Kenya) for instance, a person engaging in such sexual acts is referred to as a witch whose punishment could be death by spearing. In general, the norm for male-female relationships centres around marriage. Marriage is regarded as the sovereign regulator of sexuality. In fact, the Qur'an upholds virginity and teaches that sex is only to be enjoyed within the context of marriage. Marriage is seen as the union of persons of opposite sexes for the purposes of procreation and rearing of children. Childbearing is a religious and social duty. The African understanding of sexuality is supported by the Christian teaching on sex in marriage as a means to perpetuate God's creation, communicating love more than speech does, and making couples procreators with God (Kean, 1977). Kean's contention is that sex enables couples to understand their masculinity and femininity from a better perspective, viewing sexuality as a gift that touches human persons on all levels of existence. Contributing to the above debate, sexuality affects the physical, biological, psychological, emotional and spiritual growth of every individual at the same time, determining the manner in which people relate to themselves and to others. It is with this realisation that social groups and individuals have been supporting family planning initiatives to liberate the sexual act from procreation. Sexual union must not always lead to procreation, for if it did, then it becomes very difficult to justify sexual union among infertile partners. One of the major discussion points now concentrates upon the right of everybody to get pleasure from experiences of sexuality. This can be witnessed in the campaign to change female genital mutilation (FGM). In fact, in Africa, Kenya in particular is notorious for abuses of sex associated with gender roles and the confusion between the cultural interpretations of the female/male with femininity or masculinity which leaves one uncertain about the place of sexuality in the changing world.

4

WHAT CURRENT SEX EDUCATION IS LIKE

Sex and relationships education, like all education, is primarily the responsibility of parents. Therefore, parental authority must be maintained, such as through consultation with parents and the parental right of withdrawal from sex education.

Sex education teaching and materials that ignore biblical standards are damaging for young people and have long-term consequences for society as a whole.

Primary school is too early for the kind of sex and relationships education advocated by the sex education lobby. Some of the materials already being recommended for primary schools are completely inappropriate.

> Sex education teaching and materials that ignore biblical standards are damaging for young people and have long-term consequences for society as a whole.

Current sex education can often add to the sexualised culture by exposing even children who are protected from inappropriate material by their parents at home to explicit images and discussion topics at school. Even where controversial issues are not raised by the teachers themselves, questions asked by classmates in sex education lessons can expose children to information and discussion beyond what is suitable or age-appropriate.

PARENTAL RESPONSIBILITY

The special relationship between parents and their children is clearly seen throughout Scripture. The fifth commandment says we are to honour our father and mother (Exodus 20:12; Ephesians 6:2-3). The Bible speaks of children being a gift of God to parents (Psalm 127:3). Parenthood is given by God and parents carry a God-given authority and responsibility for the raising of children (Ephesians 6:4). This God-ordained pattern of parental authority is a general principle applying to all parents and all children.

Christian parents are to teach their children to love God (Deuteronomy 6:4-9), and children are to obey their parents because "this is right" (Ephesians 6:1) and "pleases the Lord" (Colossians 3:20). Children should listen to their fathers' instruction and not forsake their mothers' teaching (Proverbs 1:8).

So, the Bible is clear that parents have the primary responsibility for training their children. Anything that threatens to undermine this is of great concern and must be strongly resisted if Christian parents are to be able to fulfil their God-given responsibilities.

DUTY TO PROTECT YOUNG PEOPLE

There is a duty to defend the vulnerable and the weak: "Speak up for those who cannot speak for themselves, for the rights of all who are destitute. Speak up and judge fairly; defend the rights of the poor and needy" (Proverbs 31:8-9).

Jesus gave a very solemn warning of judgement for those who lead children who believe in him to sin. Jesus said,

> "It would be better for him to be thrown into the sea with a large millstone tied around his neck" (Mark 9:42).

BUILDING AN EVIDENCE- AND RIGHTS-BASED APPROACH TO HEALTHY DECISION-MAKING

As they grow up, young people face important decisions about relationships, sexuality, and sexual behaviour. The decisions they make can impact their health and well-being for the rest of their lives. Young people have the right to lead healthy lives, and society has the responsibility to prepare youth by providing them with comprehensive sexual health education that gives them the tools they need to make healthy decisions. But it is not enough for programmes to include discussions of abstinence and contraception to help young people avoid unintended pregnancy or disease. Comprehensive sexual health education must do more. It must provide young people with honest, age-appropriate information and skills necessary to help them take personal responsibility for their health and overall well-being. This paper provides an overview of research on effective sex education, laws and policies that shape it, and how it can impact young people's lives.

WHAT IS SEXUAL HEALTH EDUCATION?

Sex education is the provision of information about bodily development, sex, sexuality, and relationships, along with skills-building to help young people communicate about and make informed decisions regarding sex and their sexual health. Sex education should occur throughout a student's grade levels, with information appropriate to students' development and cultural background. It should include information about puberty and reproduction, abstinence, contraception and condoms, relationships, sexual violence prevention, body image, gender identity and sexual orientation. It should be taught by trained teachers. Sex education should be informed by evidence of what works best to prevent unintended pregnancy and sexually transmitted infections, but it should also respect young people's right to complete and honest information. Sex education should treat sexual development as a normal, natural part of human development.

SEX EDUCATION

Secular humanist defines sex education as a means by which young people are helped to protect themselves against abuse, exploitation, unintended pregnancies, STIs and HIV and AIDS through what is known as comprehensive sex education. Post-modern socialists assert that it is widely accepted that young people have a right to sex education because it aims at contributing to young people's positive experience of their sexuality by enhancing the quality of their relationships and their ability to make informed decisions over their lifetime. This implicitly teaches young people to have "safe sex," avoid pregnancy and STIs while having sex, and accept one's sexual activity. In opposition to this opinion, Armstrong asserts that sex was created by God for the mutual fellowship, enjoyment and creating of babies for married couples. Therefore, having sex outside the context God created it, undermines God's creational intent for sex, this has severe penalties. He therefore defines sex education as the comprehensive communication of the biblical principles guiding sex. This is to help young people form positive Christ-like attitudes of their sexuality.

In an era of sexual freedom, religious institutions can guide and assist its members towards surviving in the global sex culture. In the previous years, even though Ghanaian youth received no comprehensive education on either traditional principles of sex or the biblical principles of sex, there was less incidence of sexual activity and moral decay. These days, due to human rights, breakdown of cultural taboos, sexual freedom and negative influence of modern culture, so much damage has been done to morality and sexual crisis has worsened especially among young people. Consequently, there is the need to start educating the current youth on the biblical principles of sex early rather than waiting for them to attain puberty age. Various worldviews ascribe various definitions to sex which influences various sex educational programmes. The church has the theology of sex and can best educate young people with this theology. Diligence in this activity through teaching, preaching, drama, choreography, as well as discussions with young people may appropriately respond to the sex crisis.

The issue of sexuality education has become an exceptionally controversial one. The mere mention of sexuality education gives rise to many questions. But before one can ask questions there needs to be clarification and a definition must be given. Sexuality education as defined by SIECUS (Sex Information and Education Council of the U.S.) is,

> "A lifelong process of building a strong foundation for sexual health through acquiring information and forming attitudes, beliefs and values about identity, relationships, and intimacy."

This education takes place on a daily basis in homes, schools, faith-based institutions and through the media. Its curricula encompass sexual development, reproductive health, interpersonal relationships, and affection, intimacy, body image and gender roles. It is a curriculum that teaches knowledge, behaviours, attitudes and skills that promote committed family relationships, healthful relationships, good character, healthful sexuality and reproductive health. Sexuality education seeks to assist children in understanding a positive view of sexuality, provide them with the skills about taking care of their sexual health and help them to acquire skills to make decisions now and in the future.

In additoin, Sexuality education addresses the biological, socio-cultural, psychological and spiritual dimensions of sexuality from the cognitive domain (information), affective domain (feelings, values, and attitudes), and the behavioural domain (communication and decision-making skills). Such education enables the young person to know him/herself and hence relate comfortably with others. This is contrary to the misconception that sexuality education encourages sexual activities. Three (3) studies on the impact of sexuality education on a number of sexual partners found a significant decrease in partners and seven (7) studies found no impact and none found a significant increase. Once more, this is strong evidence that sexuality education programmes do not increase the number of sexual partners.

Proponents of sexuality education maintain that sexuality programmes teach: knowledge and skills of critical issues related to sexuality, e.g., intimacy, human relationships, sexual identity and gender roles, reproductive anatomy and body image, puberty and the reproductive anatomy, emotional aspects of maturation, the value of abstinence among teens who are not sexually active, alternative methods of contraception and HIV/STD prevention and the health consequences of avoiding contraceptives and prevention methods among sexually active youth. It is evident that these programmes teach so much more than sex. And as human beings, our sexuality is part of our identity. However, the plan of sexuality education includes many aspects of life not only sexual intercourse.

SEX EDUCATION BY CHURCH PASTORS

In Pentecostal churches some pastors indicate that sex education is very much needed. This is because, they believe the church offers a unique platform to educate the youth on sex. More so, the church sees the youth as the future of the church and as such, needs to invest in all aspects of their live. This corroborated the findings of Rijk van Dijk (2013) who indicated that Pentecostal movement pays much attention to the development of youths. The Pastor indicated that, "We deem sex education as important and try to fuse it at youth trainings. We want to bring our youths up well and godly."

If sex education must be taught and given much attention in the church, one pastor indicated, it should be fused into the youth meetings of the church. In an interview, the pastor confessed that in the church he was not directly involved in sex education as it is left for the elders in charge of the youths and other leaders to coordinate. Thus, the pastor was unable to tell what goes into the sex education in the church. This implies that although sex education is deemed important in the church, church pastors are not seen teaching the subject in the church as this is relegated to youth leaders to do. Pastors are messengers of God; their words carry so much weight. As such, a pastor's sex education will be much received and seen as important by the youths. It is thus important that pastors take active role in youths about sex education. This will also make the youths comfortable to approach the pastor on sex education-related issues and thus, create a bond between the youth and the pastor.

SERIOUSNESS ATTACHED TO SEX EDUCATION BY YOUTHS

The study seeks to find out how serious the youth are about sex education and the quest to making prudent choice regarding sex. The results revealed that all the youths deem sex education as very important. Sex is an integral part of human life and can affect one's relationship with God, thus, it is very encouraging to note that youths are keen to know about sex in order to make prudent choices.

The youths revealed that sex education is taught in their church. However, the youths also indicated that what is taught as sex education touches only on what sex is, why it should not be engaged in as unmarried youths and a little of sexually transmitted diseases. They also indicated however that this education is limited and happens once in a while. Interestingly, the youths revealed that more attention is given to issues on dating and courtship as against sex education. Dating and courtship are important, however, sex education is more important because whether dating or courting, youths can be tempted to have sex and as such, must be educated on it and prepared to make prudent choices. This implies that not all issues related to sex and not all questions related to sex are tackled at the church. If done well and given topmost priority, sex education in the church will stop youths from seeking knowledge elsewhere and will contribute to prudent morality within the youth in the church.

On how serious sex education is to the youths, majority of the youths indicated that they pay much attention to sex education. It is thus, a good sign that youths of the church are not silent on issues of sex and are serious about learning about it. Sex affects the spiritual lives of people if not done in a godly way and thus, there is a need to teach youths about sex and for them to take keen interest in learning godly sexual orientations.

IMPACT OF SEX EDUCATION

On the impact of sex education, it was found out that the sex education is not yielding the desired result. The presiding Pastor indicated that though the church holds sex education programmes (limited however), there are still records of sexual misconduct amongst the youth of the church. These included teenage pregnancy, pregnancy before marriage, and reported active sex lives amongst youths. The Pastor attributed these to the exposure of youths to the internet and social media.

On the part of the youths, they indicated that the sex education given at church is less frequent and shallow. Thus, they resort to other platforms to learn more about sex. This implies that the level of sex education in the church is inadequate and does not really fit the needs of the youths. This accounts for the youths seeking for more knowledge on sex education outside the church.

All the youths and the Pastor indicated that they will recommend sex education to other churches. However, the youths indicated that more on sex education should be taught and all curious questions asked at the church so that the youths will not seek knowledge on sex from other sources that might mislead them.

CAUSES OF SEXUAL IMMORALITY AND ITS EFFECTS

The major conclusion drawn from this study is that, sex education is very important and needs serious attention from the general public and the church. Students in elementary and secondary schools, as well as vocational schools, apprenticeship programmes, colleges and universities can be victims of sexual harassment because of lack of sex education.

Several studies suggest that sex education is more needed in non-nurturing environmental and familial contexts such as poor parent-child relationships and family stress (Meyerson, Long, Miranda & Marx, 2002; Brown et al., 1999). It is no doubt that many of the youth from such homes and environment will have their share of sex education in the church.

Lack of parental care also contributes to lack of sex education. This is mostly as a result of lack of education and the problem of unemployment by parents. According to Chege et al. (1994), for students to survive in school, they accept gifts which potentially lend them to be victims of sexual abuse, in other words, lack of basic needs therefore acts as a cause that creates conducive atmosphere for student sexual harassment in schools and the community. They therefore need to provide the needed sex education for such vulnerable people.

The church may have a problem of time to give enough sex education to members but the fact is arrangement should be made to create times for the members for such purposes, especially the youth.

The study has found out that there are several negative effects of lack of sex education. Some of the effects from the study are:

- social vices,
- school dropout,
- poor academic performance,
- low moral standards,
- loss of self-esteem,
- low productivity,
- stigmatisation, among others.

Instead of changing, many believers try to reconcile their lifestyle of free sex and cohabitation with the Christian faith.

5
COHABITATION

The different values and attitudes regarding relationships and sexuality maintained in the same culture and family are remarkable. It often results in drastic differences between parents and children, and usually cause immense stress and sometimes even separation between them (Noëth 2010:14). It also happens that parents, for the sake of peace, just discard their own views, or approve of the present view of free sex and cohabitation. There are even those parents who participate in this lifestyle.

These different values are certainly not something new. In Christ's conversation with the Samaritan woman, it seems that she was involved in a cohabitating relationship. Jesus said:

> "The fact is, you have had five husbands, and the man you now have is not your husband" (John 4:18).

This lifestyle was especially propagated during the 1960s and 1970s with rock 'n' roll, hippies and the playboy ideology. However, in our present society, these views have increased in popularity, and the pendulum still swings in the same direction. This is also true in most Western societies:

> "Since the 1970s the incidence of cohabitation has increased sharply in many Western societies. In Britain, for example, cohabitation before marriage had become the majority practice by 1992" (Jenkins 1995:238).

Nevertheless, with each extreme view and lifestyle, there are negative consequences for individuals as well as for all of society.

Unfortunately, most Christians find it difficult to give account of the biblical view in this regard. The result is that they submit to peer pressure, or just give way to their own desires. After all, we live in a world where television programmes promote it, commercials advertise it, Hollywood glamorises it, parents tolerate it, and churches ignore it—what a combination! In terms of the media.

One of the greatest factors appears to be the media. The average teen watches twenty-three hours of television per week. As Proverbs 23:7 says,

> "For as he thinks in his heart, so is he."

If inappropriate information is fed into the brain, then inappropriate responses will result. If young people are exposed to sexually explicit types of behaviour via the media, they are more likely to act out that behaviour (Hagar 2000: 209).

Instead of changing, many believers try to reconcile their lifestyle of free sex and cohabitation with the Christian faith. It is usually done by rationalising and justifying it, or by trying to convince others that their behaviour is acceptable and appropriate before God. Schenck (1999: 55) rightfully declares that such behaviour boils down to a disregard of the third commandment:

> "You shall not misuse the name of the Lord your God, for the Lord will not hold anyone guiltless who misuses his name" (Exodus 20:7).

He explains that when we claim God's approval about something that is clearly not his will, or when we claim his direction for something that is of our own making, we actually misrepresent Him and take his name in vain. We illegitimately lend the imprimatur of God's good name to something that is not good, which is tantamount to a fraudulent claim endorsement.

Accordingly, this issue has become an increasing crisis in our society. Research (Van Wyk 2009: 85) also indicates that the majority of cases of cohabitation originated from a background of broken families. In South Africa, 64% of first marriages end up in divorce, 82% of second marriages, and 91% of third marriages. Cohabitation seems to be a symptom of deeper problems (mainly man's relationship with God and broken families), and these issues need urgent attention.

More so, because most preachers remain silent and do not give church members clear biblical direction. Usually, they remain silent out of fear that certain members (sometimes prominent members) will take exception to such preaching. Their silence, however, seems to cause many people's lives to be dominated by anxiety, feelings of guilt, sin and confusion.

The silence of the church correlates of course with the popular and also secular view that we should not be judgmental in this regard. If, however, it is maintained that an individual has the right to determine his or her own moral standards, and other people or the Bible has no right to condemn them, then also the church has no right to say anything about cohabitation. Sometimes the church does not even have anything to say about it!

It will be a sad day if the church loses its prophetic message. Such a church will, from a biblical perspective, be irrelevant to society (Vorster 2010: 9). The church has a message that does not only speak of God's grace, but also of his condemnation. If this is no longer the case, then the church has reached a situation as described by Paul in 2 Timothy 4:3-4.

> "For the time will come when men will not put up with sound doctrine. Instead, to suit their own desires, they will gather around them a great number of teachers to say what their itching ears want to hear. They will turn their ears away from truth and turn aside to myths."

This does not mean that the application of biblical principles as such can solve the problem. The biblical message should always be communicated in love and understanding

(Noëth 2010: 15). Nevertheless, principles alone cannot really change a person's life. Therefore, the emphasis should not only be on what the Bible says, but also on why the Bible says it. And even that is not enough. Biblical principles concerning morality presuppose a loving relationship with God. Without such a relationship, no profound change is possible. Obeying biblical principles should always be the result of a relationship with God, and not something that is done coercively.

Christian couples that cohabitate, experience conflict in their relationship with God, or are in general careless about it, they do not really love Him (Noëth 2010: 15). This carelessness and lack of love for God is in fact at the core of their problem. Jesus said in John 14:23-24,

> "If anyone loves me, he will obey my teaching. My Father will love him, and we will come to him and make our home with him. He who does not love me will not obey my teaching. These words you hear are not my own; they belong to the Father who sent me."

WHAT CONSTITUTES A MARRIAGE AGAINST COHABITATION?

To understand what is fundamental to marriage and what constitutes it, we have to go back to those principles of scripture when God instituted marriage. This foundation is laid in mainly two references from the book of Genesis (other scriptures in this regard will be dealt with later).

Genesis 1:27-28,

> "So God created man in his own image, in the image of God he created him; male and female He created them. God blessed them and said to them: 'Be fruitful and increase in number . . .'"

Also Genesis 2:24:

> "For this reason a man will leave his father and mother and be united to his wife, and they will become one flesh."

In the New Testament Jesus also referred to these verses in order to emphasise what is fundamental to marriage, we read in Matthew 19:4-6,

> "Haven't you read", he replied, "that in the beginning the Creator 'made them male and female' and said, 'For this reason a man will leave his father and mother and be united to his wife, and the two will become one flesh?' So they are no longer two, but one. Therefore, what God has joined together, let man not separate."

HE CREATED THEM (MALE AND FEMALE) IN HIS OWN IMAGE

The image of God is, among other things, also realised in the relationship between man and woman. This relationship finds its climax in a marriage that reflects something of the image of God in the sense that the love, closeness, peace and harmony that exist between the Father, Son and Holy Spirit are mirrored in the relationship of the husband and wife:

> "We are created in this image, to live with the qualities that mark the Trinity: love, intimacy and community. This is why it was not good for the man to be alone. In his aloneness, he didn't mirror the image of the triune God" (Stanton & Maier 2005: 173).

Marriage is therefore particularly healing in a society where lovelessness, loneliness, stress and separation are causing so much grief and pain.

In this bond of one man and one woman, in a heterosexual relationship, God's image is expressed further by the fertility of man and woman, and the accompanying potential to beget children. After all, children and parenthood reflect also something of the image of God as realised in the relationship between God the Father and his Son Jesus Christ.

The more the image of God is realised in a person's life, the more a person becomes what God intended him or her to be. It is something that cannot be separated from God's love for us. It is a love in which God grants us to experience more and more of who He is, and in this process He also uses marriage and family as instruments to realise it. This makes marriage and family an exercise field to develop into a direction where God can restore his image in our lives. To be like God means in the first instance that true love, as realised in the ultimate marriage between Christ and his bride (the church), is also realised in the lives of married couples. That is also true in the relationship between parents and children as seen in the relationship between the Father and his Son Jesus Christ. In other words, marriage and family receive from God an eternal dimension.

This deeper meaning of the husband-wife relationship is totally missed in a cohabiting relationship. It is a shallow relationship with no eternal dimension at all. It is a relationship that is built upon one's own satisfaction and fulfilment, and therefore egocentric in nature. God's given goal of marriage is missed and the focus is on what I can get out of the relationship rather than on what I can give (Van Wyk 2009: 85). Almost nothing of spiritual intimacy actualises, and therefore the image of God, in terms of the relationship between

Father, Son and Holy Spirit, is not reflected. In fact, a lack of spiritual intimacy enhances loneliness and separation within a relationship.

Cohabitation is furthermore not directed to the eternal marriage between Christ and his bride, it is in a dead end with almost no meaning. It is not an exercise field like marriage, in which man is prepared for eternity. It is therefore not instrumental in God's hands to help man to be restored to his image (different from animals) and to transcend that which is transient and mundane. We should realise that if a person's life lacks eternal values, he or she will increasingly be confronted with the meaningless and emptiness of such a life.

Friendship relationships help unmarried people to experience something of that which is pre-eminently experienced in a married relationship. Contrary to this, cohabitation is not a friendship relationship as realised in marriage or in general. It cannot be a marriage-friendship because there is no marriage, and friendship out of wedlock respects the other person's privacy and space, whilst this is not done in cohabiting relationships. When they are sexually together, they claim each other's space and want to share in the privileges of a marriage-friendship without any commitment. Such intimacy does not enhance friendship, but rather destroys it — it is an inherent contradictory. They overstep the boundaries of friendship and simultaneously push one another away (no commitment).

As far as family is concerned, cohabiters are in general hesitant to have children. Research shows for example, that abortion on demand is much higher amongst women who are in a cohabiting relationship than in a married one (Ambert 2005: 2). This is due to the uncertainty of their relationship, and the risk to become a single parent. Most women are obviously not prepared to take such a risk. Reproduction is part of God's plan with marriage, but for cohabiters such an idea is couched in uncertainty and threat. This uncertainty and threat might be transferred to a later marriage, so that they decide not to have any children at all.

A man will leave his father and mother and be united to his wife.

The statement that a man should leave his father and mother and be united to his wife is a clear indication that God instituted marriage. It is not a cultural institution. Therefore, leaving your family to establish another is at the heart of marriage.

Women help men become what they are created to be, and men help women become what they are created to be. To deny this is to deny our full, God-given humanity. Men and women need each other, and marriage is where we most fully and completely come together (Stanton & Maier 2005: 173-174).

Flanagan and Williams (2011) emphasise the fact that when a husband and wife are united in marriage, it is also something that becomes known to the rest of the family and friends. It is a public event that is solemnised before witnesses, and therefore others in society are involved.

The message is clear, they have committed themselves to each other by pledging certain vows, and are no longer available to anyone else.

Though vows are not explicitly mentioned in Scripture, they are implicit in the idea of 'cleave' or be 'united.' Wedding vows have two functions:

1) to define the nature of the relationship; and 2) to declare future intent. Whilst marriage is a commitment for the future as well as for the present, cohabitation tends to be a relationship just for the present with the future left deliberately open-ended (Jenkins 1995: 238).

Marriage is therefore a commitment that is made regardless of what conflict or stress may develop. In most aspects of the relationship it is no longer about me but about us deciding, feeling, planning and living a particular lifestyle (Möller 2000: 14). This is the secure environment into which children are later born, nurtured and allowed to grow up as adults.

Opposed to this, cohabitation is a private agreement between a man and woman, which often disregards the wishes of the other. No public vows of commitment are made, and no witnesses are involved. In other words, uncertainty regarding the permanency of the relationship is from the beginning part of it. It is expected that the relationship will not last for long, and it offers least of all a safe and stable environment into which children can be born or reared.

He will be united to his wife, and they will become one flesh.

When Christ referred to Genesis 2:24, ". . . be united to his wife, and they will become one flesh . . ." His conclusion was: Matthew 19:6 ". . . So they are no longer two, but one."

To be one flesh refers to physical or sexual unity between husband and wife, but it is also more than that. The sexual relationship between man and woman is placed in a broader framework, the unity of marriage—be united to his wife. He is first united to his wife (spiritually), and then they become one flesh. A sexual relationship does not really bring unity; it rather presupposes unity. It is a celebration of the unity that already exists, and through sexuality this unity is accentuated and made more intense.

The biblical view of marriage is that husband and wife should be one spiritually and physically, and that physical unity should realise in the context of spiritual unity. Heyns (1986: 160) accentuates that in this unity, faithful love should be seen as the highest norm in their relationship. After all, marriage that presupposes oneness and faithfulness between a man and a woman is still a marriage even if there may for some reason be no sexual intimacy (sickness, biological problems, impotency, aging, etc.). It is not sexuality as such, but marriage (and the accompanying commitment, love and faithfulness) that makes them one so that they are no longer two, but one person.

In a cohabiting relationship there exists an indifference regarding sexuality. It is acceptable for them to have a sexual relationship without true spiritual unity and commitment.

In a cohabiting agreement this unity is not recognised and man and woman keep their surnames. By this they accentuate the fact that they have remained two separate individuals. No new family relationships are established (father- or mother- or son- or daughter-in-law), and the wishes and desires of parents and other family are usually ignored. It again accentuates the self-centred nature of such relationships.

COHABITATION AND THE LAW

A marriage certificate refers to the fact that a man and a woman are lawfully married. This legal aspect of marriage is also found in the Bible. The couple and the parents from both sides, made an agreement together concerning the future marital commitment (Möller 2000: 5). This was a legal agreement that laid certain responsibilities on both the parents and the couple. For example, marriage was seen as an agreement or covenant between man and wife that involved absolute faithfulness as implied in Proverbs 2:17, Ezekiel 16:8 and Malachi 2:15-16. It also meant that the couple was married in public to ensure that there could be no doubt that the man and the woman were lawfully wed (Judges 14:1-20; John 2:1-12).

In the New Testament marriage receives further meaning. It is seen as much more than a mere transaction between a man and a woman (Vorster 2010:11). In Ephesians 5:22-33 it is said that the relationship is built upon the relationship between Christ and his church and presupposes mutual and unconditional love for one another. The different roles of husband and wife are stipulated and in 1 Corinthians 7:5 Paul says that a couple should not refuse sexual intimacy because it might lead to temptations and a lack of self-control.

These responsibilities also meant that the husband could not easily divorce his wife. Divorce could only be realised if it was confirmed by a legal document. After all, a legal relationship can only be broken by another legal regulation. Here the Bible refers to a letter of divorce that should be handed to the wife in case of marital separation (Deuteronomy 24:1; Matthew 19:7). It was a letter that was compiled and approved by the elders who divorced the couple legally from each other.

Therefore, marriage has according to the Bible, a religious as well as a legal aspect that should be honoured. It is something that corresponds with Paul's pronouncements in Romans 13:1-2:

> "Everyone must submit himself to the governing authorities, for there is no authority except that which God has established. The authorities that exist have been established by God. Consequently, he who rebels against the authority is rebelling against what God has instituted, and those who do so will bring judgment on themselves."

THE MESSAGE AND OUTCOME OF COHABITATION

Cohabitation refers in this context to an unmarried couple that lives together like a married couple. The motive in doing so is usually to make absolutely sure that they are compatible before they engage in marriage. It is also possible that they do not foresee any marriage at all and reject this institution completely. In such cases cohabitation is seen as an experiment to test their compatibility to be a couple — and if they are still young, to determine whether it is suitable for them to have children or not.

Cohabitation has become socially acceptable (even amongst some Christians) although it is contrary to the most fundamental teachings of the Christian faith. This acceptance is reflected in the way we have changed our language in this regard. Flanigan and Williams (2011) point out that the term partner is presently used without any differentiation between cohabiting partners and married partners.

Nevertheless, to see cohabitation as an alternative for marriage is a total misconception of what marriage is all about. A couple that makes a marital commitment, does so with the full understanding that they have chosen each other completely, and with the intention to engage in a lifelong relationship. Against this, cohabiters keep from the very start, a back door open to make sure that there is always a convenient escape route if things do not work out between them.

Hereby it is not denied that divorce can also be seen as an escape route for married couples. However, in the case of cohabiting couples, separation is much easier in terms of responsibilities towards each other, and the possibility of such a separation, in contrast to marriage, is part of the relationship from the very beginning. It is therefore a relationship in which they have not chosen each other completely.

A valid question is: Is cohabitation still not a better option than marriage? Is it not better to have an open back door, and to make sure that the relationship will indeed be a success? In theory, it sounds good and logical, but in practice, it is not the case. There are certain reasons for that.

CONFLICTING COMMUNICATION

A cohabiting couple communicates to each other, a double and conflicting message. It is a way of communication that is very confusing. The classic example is that of the mother who says to her child: "I've told you a million times, never exaggerate!" Such a double and conflicting message is also communicated when a parent says something but does the opposite. After all, one does not only communicate with words, but also with one's deeds. Therefore, to forbid your child to lie, but then do it yourself, is a further example of double and conflicting communication. In fact, non-verbal communication speaks with more authority than words. Your behaviour and deeds are more credible than what you say.

THE DANGERS CONCERNING COHABITATION

Some research has already been conducted in terms of the outcomes concerning cohabitation, as well as the effect it has on the children involved. Anne-Marie Ambert (2005: 2) has made a study of the results of many research papers that examined the social, emotional and financial effects of cohabitation and marriage on men, women, children and society. Some of the outcomes are as follows:

- Some individuals choose cohabitation because it does not require sexual fidelity. Evidence indicates that the experience of a less-committed cohabitation shapes subsequent marital behaviour.

- Some couples continue to live their marriage through the perspective of the insecurity, lack of pooling of resources, low commitment level, and even lack of fidelity of their prior cohabitation.

- Married couples that previously lived together are less faithful in their sexual lives. And a lack of fidelity is known to be a factor leading to higher rates of marriage breakdown.

- Married couples that had cohabitated had less positive problem-solving behaviours and were, on average, less supportive of each other than those who had not cohabited.

- Couples who had cohabited before marriage had much higher rates of premarital violence than those who had not lived together. This premarital violence then lead to higher rates of marital violence, another factor related to divorce.

- Those who cohabit are generally more approving of divorce as a solution to marital problems.

- Couples who cohabit are less religious than those who marry without prior cohabitation. On this point there are several studies that indicate a correlation between religiosity and marital happiness as well as stability.

- A propensity to cohabit soon after starting a romantic relationship leads to a pattern of instability. People who go through a series of *de facto* relationships are more likely to contract quick marriages, which are harder to remain faithful to.

- A risk factor with cohabitation is its unstable nature. Most unions dissolve within five years.

- In the United States an estimated 40% of all children will live with their single mother (never-married or divorced) and her boyfriend at some point before their 16th birthday.

- For children, cohabitation means a greater risk of living within an unstable family structure, especially when their mother cohabits with a man who is not their father. Such children have lower school performance and more behavioural problems.

- Cohabitation affects the mother's capacity to give adequate attention to children, and contributes to general neglect. The mother's partner is not likely to compensate for this deficiency because his attachment to the children is often low.

- Physical abuse is also more likely and young children in cohabiting relationships are more likely to be injured or killed by their mother's live-in boyfriend than in biological families. Girls, for their part, are at higher risk of being sexually abused.

- Commitment and stability are at the core of children's needs: yet, in a great proportion of cohabitations, these two requirements are absent.

At the end of her study, Ambert notes, that many people maintain that marriage is merely a matter of lifestyle choice and that it is equivalent to cohabitation, but most research rejects this point of view. Marriage is, in fact, beneficial to both spouses and children. Lawmakers should take these outcomes into consideration.

CONCLUSION

Research supports the view that the escalation of cohabitation has extremely negative consequences on character development, relationships and the basic structures of society. Parents, young people and children are in general uninformed concerning the dangers involved in cohabitation. This lack of knowledge results in a situation where the whole issue of cohabitation is not really communicated amongst parents and children. This leads to a situation where arguments concerning free sex and cohabitation are mainly dealt with on an emotional level that triggers much conflict and separation.

To be informed, to know and to be able to communicate all the consequences of cohabitation is therefore urgent. To tell the truth about cohabitation is of course not always the popular route to follow. Cohabitants do not always want to hear the truth, but as Adams (1973) puts it:

> "Of course the truth hurts, but it never hurts like a lie. Sin always causes pain and misery. But repentance leads to peace. When you tell the truth, the hurt

> comes quickly, but healing soon follows. If you put off telling the truth, you will suffer longer and in the end suffer the pain of facing it after all. When one wrongly handles the truth, it really hurts" (p. 396).

However, telling the truth is not enough. Sin and disobedience to God's principles are not overcome by good argumentation or logic. Sin is an adventure on its own, it has a fascination and stubbornness that ignores all good argumentation, logic and truth. Paul, for example, wrote to the Galatians who had turned from the way of truth and said:

> "You foolish Galatians! Who has bewitched you?" (Gal 3:1).

6

SOURCES OF SEXUALITY EDUCATION

Sexuality education aims to develop and strengthen the ability of children and young people to make conscious, satisfying, healthy and respectful choices regarding relationships, sexuality and emotional and physical health. Sexuality education does not encourage children to have but rather to stay chaste.

Have you ever asked yourself from where do young people learn about sexuality? The fact is, sexuality education begins at home. Parents and caregivers are and ought to be the primary sexuality educators of their children. Teachable moments and opportunities to discuss sexuality issues with children occur on a daily basis.

> Young people also learn about sexuality from other sources. These include friends, teachers, neighbours, television, music, books, and magazines, advertisement and the internet.

From the moment of birth, children learn about love through touch, and relationships. Infants learn about sexuality when their parents talk to them, dress them, show affection, play with them, and teach them the names of the parts of their bodies. And as children grow into adolescence, they continue to receive messages about sexual behaviours, attitudes and values from their families and within their social environment. Some parents and caregivers are comfortable discussing sexuality issues with their children. Other parents feel anxious about providing too much information or are embarrassed about not knowing answers to questions that children ask.

Honest, open communication between parents and children through childhood, the pre-teen years, adolescence, and young adulthood can help lay the foundation for young people to mature into sexually healthy adults. Young people also learn about sexuality from other sources. These include friends, teachers, neighbours, television, music, books, and magazines, advertisement and the internet. These things will bring increasing pressures for young people. It is established that 50% of internet sites concern sex. Perhaps we could begin to think of sexual pleasure as a human right. Children also frequently learn through planned opportunities in faith communities, community-based agencies and schools.

WHAT ARE THE BENEFITS OF SEXUALITY EDUCATION?

Sexuality education delivered within a safe and enabling learning environment and alongside access to health services has a positive and lifelong effect on the health and well-being of young people.

Studies in several European countries have shown that the introduction of longer national sexuality education programmes has led to a reduction in teenage pregnancies and abortions and a decline in rates of sexually transmitted infections (STIs) and HIV infection among young people aged 15-24 years. Beyond that, by increasing confidence and strengthening skills to deal with different challenges, sexuality education can empower young people to develop stronger and/or meaningful relationships.

Social norms and gender inequality influence the expression of sexuality and sexual behaviour. Many young women have low levels of power or control in their sexual relationships.

Young men, on the other hand, may feel pressure from their peers to act according to all sexual stereotypes and engage in controlling or harmful behaviours. Good quality sexuality education has a positive impact on attitudes and values and can even oust the power dynamics in intimate relationships, thus contributing to the prevention of abuse and fostering mutually respectful and consensual partnerships.

THE IMPORTANCE OF GOING BEYOND INFORMAL SEXUALITY EDUCATION

Various social and technical developments during the past decades have triggered the need for good quality sexuality education, which can enable young people to deal with their sexuality in a safe and satisfactory manner. Examples of these kind of developments are: globalisation and the arrival of new population groups with different cultural and religious backgrounds; the rapid spread of new media, particularly the Internet, Internet pornography and mobile phone technology; the emergence of HIV and AIDS; increasing concerns about STIs, abortion, infertility and the sexual abuse of children and adolescents; and, last but not least, changing attitudes towards sexuality and changing sexual behaviour among young people. Formalised sexuality education, as opposed to peer education and extra-curricular activities, is well placed to reach a majority of children and young people.

Parents, relatives, friends and other laypersons are important sources of learning about human relationships and sexuality, especially for younger age groups. However, informal sources are often insufficient, because of the complexity of knowledge and skills required when discussing about topics such as contraception, STIs, emotional development and communication.

CONCLUSION

God gives us very clear guidance in His Word on how we can best experience the gift of intimacy and love that He gave to us through sex. If you are wondering what the Bible says about premarital sex or marital sex, use the verses below to study in context what God would have for you to learn. Sex was meant as a wonderful experience between husband and wife to provide physical, emotional and spiritual bonding.

If you are feeling overwhelmed with a sexual sin, remember that God promises to forgive us and cleanse us from all unrighteousness (1 John 1:9). God wants to pour grace on you so you can move forward in healing from hurtful sexual choices and into a place of fulfilment!

REFERENCES

Adams, J. E., 1973, The Christian counselor's manual, Baker Book House, Grand Rapids, Michigan.

Ambert, A., 2005, 'Cohabitation: A recipe for marital ruin', Zenith Daily Dispatch, 17 September, n.p.

Flanagan, D. & Williams, E. S., 2011, Cohabitation or marriage, viewed 07 January 2011, from http://www.belmonthouse.co.uk/Marriage,%20cohab%20and%20divorce/cohabitation.htm

Gardner, E. C., 1975, s.v. 'New Testament Ethics', in J. Macquarrie (ed.), A Dictionary of Christian Ethics, Flechter & Son Ltd, Norwich, pp. 229-232.

Hagar, W. D., 2000, 'Casualties of the sexual revolution', in J. F. Kilner, P. C. Cunningham & W. D. Hagar (eds.), Youth risk takers, The reproduction revolution, A Christian appraisal of sexuality, reproductive technologies, and the family, pp. 205-229.

Heyns, J. A., 1986, Teologiese Etiek, deel 2, NG Kerkboekhandel, Pretoria.

Hillerstrom, P. R., 2004, The intimacy cover-up, Kregel Publications, Grand Rapids, Michigan.

Jenkins, G. J., 1995, s.v. 'Cohabitation', in D. J. Atkinson & D. H. Field (eds.), New dictionary of Christian ethics and pastoral theology, Inter-Varsity Press, Leicester, pp. 238-239.

Louw, D. J., 1985, Die volwasse huwelik, Butterworth, Durban.

Möller, F. P., 2000, Die huwelik, Christelike etiek, vol. 8, Semper Nova Publishers, Johannesburg.

Noëth, J. G., 2010, 'As ons jongmense saamwoon' [When our young people live together], Die Kerkblad.

Schenck, R. L., 1999, The ten words that will change a nation, Albury Publishing, Tulsa, Oklahoma.

Stanton, G. T. & Maier, B., 2005, Marriage on trial, Christian Art Publishers, Vereeniging.

Thielicke, H., 1964, The ethics of sex, James Clarke and Co. Ltd., London.

Van Wyk, J., 2009, Kerklike sanksie vir saamwoon? Die 50 grootste geloofsvrae, Carpe Diem Media,

Vorster, N., 2010, 'Trou of sommer saamwoon?' [Marraige or simply live together?], Die Kerkblad, 112(3233), 9-11.

William B. Eerdmans Publishing Company, Grand Rapids, Michigan.

PERSONAL NOTES

www.ingramcontent.com/pod-product-compliance
Lightning Source LLC
LaVergne TN
LVHW050559160826
845677LV00011B/2376